Mastering Bitcoin for Beginners

----- ᴥᴥᴥ -----

The only guide for Bitcoin enthusiasts, Bitcoin investors, Bitcoin traders, Bitcoin miners and Bitcoin merchants.

James J Foskey

Text Copyright © James J Foskey

All rights reserved. No part of this guide may be reproduced in any form without permission in writing from the publisher except in the case of brief quotations embodied in critical articles or reviews.

Legal & Disclaimer

The information contained in this book and its contents is not designed to replace or take the place of any form of medical or professional advice; and is not meant to replace the need for independent medical, financial, legal or other professional advice or services, as may be required. The content and information in this book have been provided for educational and entertainment purposes only.

The content and information contained in this book have been compiled from sources deemed reliable, and it is accurate to the best of the Author's knowledge, information, and belief. However, the Author cannot guarantee its accuracy and validity and cannot be held liable for any errors and/or omissions. Further, changes are periodically made to this book as and when needed. Where appropriate and/or necessary, you must consult a professional (including but not limited to your doctor, attorney, financial advisor or such other professional advisor) before using any of the suggested remedies, techniques, or information in this book.

Upon using the contents and information contained in this book, you agree to hold harmless the Author from and against any damages, costs, and expenses, including any legal fees potentially resulting from the application of any of the information provided by this book. This disclaimer applies to any loss, damages or injury caused by the use and application, whether directly or indirectly, of any advice or information presented, whether for breach of contract, tort, negligence, personal injury, criminal intent, or under any other cause of action.

You agree to accept all risks of using the information presented inside this book.

You agree that by continuing to read this book, where appropriate and/or necessary, you shall consult a professional (including but not limited to your doctor, attorney, or financial advisor or such other advisor as needed) before using any of the suggested remedies, techniques, or information in this book.

About the Author

James J Foskey had a formal education in computer science from Stanford University and graduated at the age of 23. He currently lives and works in the Silicon Valley as a Finance technology consultant. As a Fin-tech consultant, he had worked with high caliber individual within the Silicon Valley and had built up a new P2P lending platform from scratch.

He is a technologist and serial Bitcoin writer who has become one of the most well-respected figures in Bitcoin forum for the past few years.

He is the co-founder of the bitcoin community The Cryptocurrency block. As an avid public speaker to advocate on the subject of cryptocurrency, the blockchain, Bitcoin and Ethereum, so James like to make such complex subject accessible and easy to his audience. Just as this book aims to demystify Bitcoin and the technology behind it.

James believes any average person should be able to adapt to the emerging Bitcoin while will impact everyone life.

He believes that we are living in a time when opportunities are all over the place and we ought to improve our lives by enriching our lives by reading more.

James trust blockchain will be the future of all financial market while Bitcoin could be the next pot of gold that is residing within us. He's proud to be the author of this book, and he hopes he can share some of his excitement as he journeys with us towards the next digital currency revolution.

Table of Contents

Chapter 1: What is Bitcoin?.....................1

   1.1 How does Bitcoin get "generated "? 2

   1.2 What is behind the Bitcoin technology? 3

   1.3 The Origin of Cryptocurrency – Cryptography................................. 3

   1.4 The birth of Bitcoin 4

   1.5 Bitcoin recognized as a currency 8

   1.6 Cryptocurrency debunked 12

   1.7 Cryptocurrency hashing 13

   1.8 Bitcoin hashing...................................... 13

   1.9 What is Bitcoin block?........................... 14

   1.10 Blockchain explained........................... 15

Chapter 2: Should You Invest in Bitcoin?... 17

   2.1 Why invest in Bitcoin?...........................19

   2.2 What does it really mean to invest in Bitcoin? 22

   2.3 How Bitcoins exchange operates 26

   2.4 How does a regular Bitcoin exchange really works? 27

   2.5 How Bitcoin exchange works............... 32

2.6 Buying Bitcoin from ATM 35

Chapter 3: Bitcoin Mining 39

3.1 Introducing Bitcoin Mining 39

3.2 Understanding how Bitcoin mining works 42

3.3 The 22% balance mining 43

3.4 Calculating mining profit 44

3.5 ASIC mining hardware comparison 48

3.6 Calculating non-specialized hardware for Bitcoin mining 50

3.7 Choosing Bitcoin ASIC Bitcoin miner hardware commonly used 53

Chapter 4: Bitcoin Wallet 55

4.1 What is the private key? 56

4.2 Different type of Bitcoin wallet 57

4.3 Cold Wallets and its advantage 62

4.4 Explaining Bitcoin address 63

4.5 Bitcoin address balance 64

4.6 Fun exercise to create a new Bitcoin paper wallet 66

Chapter 5: Bitcoin Mining Pool 69

5.1 Choosing a Mining Pool 70

5.2 Type of mining pool payout 72

5.3 Slushpool mining 73

5.4 Antpool mining 77

Chapter 6: Mining Hardware 81

6.1 ANTminer S9 82

Chapter 7: Bitcoin Usage 87

7.1 Your brick and mortar store 88

7.2 Fly with Bitcoin 89

7.3 Gambling with Bitcoin 91

7.4 Bitcoin trading with rare metal 91

7.5 Trading Bitcoins for shopping gift card 92

7.6 Converting your Bitcoin to cash through Bitcoin ATM 93

7.7 Shopping Bitcoins' Search engine 94

7.8 Donating your Bitcoin for charitable cause 95

7.8 How to be a Bitcoin merchant 97

Chapter 8: Bitcoin Sutra 103

Chapter 9: Conclusion 109

Chapter 1:

What is Bitcoin?

So... Bitcoin is a new type of currency, a digital currency? Just like your Dollar ($), your Pound (£), your Euro (€), your Yen(¥) and Bitcoin mined not from gold or silver but instead from code. In short, Bitcoin is an encrypted string of data or a hash, to signify one unit of currency and given to miners for their work.

In brief, Bitcoin is an innovative internet protocol created by the pseudonymous Satoshi Nakamoto that had enables value to be transferred over a communication channel. Transactions require no middlemen so anyone can transfer money anywhere in the world without using any centralized services like a bank or internet facilities like PayPal or credit card merchants like Visa or MasterCard

Mastering Bitcoin for Beginners

Bitcoins are cryptocurrency that you can send through the internet compared to other alternatives currency. Bitcoins are transferred directly from person to person via the network without going through a bank or clearing house which means end user pays lesser fees and individuals or organization can not freeze such account.

1.1 How does Bitcoin get "generated "?

Bitcoins are generated all over the internet by anybody running a free application call Bitcoin miner. Mining requires a certain amount of work for each block of coins. These amounts are automatically adjusted by the network such that bitcoins are always generated at a predicted and limited rate. Your bitcoins are stored in your digital wallet which might look familiar if you're using online banking when you transfer bitcoins, an electronic signature is added after a few minutes that transactions are verified by a miner and permanently and anonymously stored in the network.

Bitcoins are mined regularly and distributed among participating miners. They are then exchanged, bought, and sold like commodities through a mercantile system that spans the globe

Chapter 1: What is Bitcoin?

The bitcoin software is completely open source and anybody can review the source code. Bitcoin is shaping the financial industry the same way the web changed when everyone now has access to a global market.

1.2 What is behind the Bitcoin technology?

Simply put, the blockchain is the shared public ledger on which the entire decentralized distributed peer-to-peer Bitcoin network lies. All confirmed transactions are included in the blockchain so that the bitcoin wallet can calculate the spendable balance and new transactions can be verified between peer-to-peer.

To make it safer than the transferred value is verified, the digital sign transactions will provide a mathematical proof that they are valid. The integrity and the chronological order of the block chain are enforced with cryptography.

1.3 The Origin of Cryptocurrency – Cryptography

Let's take a walk back to memory lane. But first, does Cryptograph a bell to you?

Cryptography has been existence and in use for thousands of years as a way to hide secret messages. The earliest known fact of cryptography is known as Caesar cipher, a substitution of Cipher text. In Cipher cryptography, a character is substituted with by another character to form the cipher text. One of the prominent usages of cryptography is being used by Caesar to communicate between his generals by simply shifting the message to be sent by a number or letters of alphabets in his text.

Bitcoins or any digital currency adapt to cryptography which explains why Bitcoin is also known as cryptocurrencies because they use a digital signature to take a process further by providing the sender to send the message when the sender can't reject because it was initiated by them.

1.4 The birth of Bitcoin

Let's now fast forward to current century and walk through the history and the evolvement of Bitcoin.

Chapter 1: What is Bitcoin?

The birth of Bitcoin (2008)

In 2008, the aftermath subprime mortgage crisis led to quantitative easing by the federal reserve, global recession and the European sovereign debt-crisis which led to dropping of confidence in government issued currencies.

It was this perfect storm for the emergence of a new type of crypto currency, Bitcoin.

Since the birth of the internet, there have been movements to create virtual cash. However, earlier attempts could not solve the "double spending "problem. What do I mean by double spending? Double spending means in short if digital money is just information, the very same information can be duplicated and spend twice or more.

The way around to this double spending problem is to verify whether a token has been spent or not by a trusted source. While a central authority which is usually a bank in the real world, it also creates weakness in that system by having a single breaking point.

The innovation phase (2008 to 2009)

Bitcoin bypasses this by using the block chain, which is a public ledger of transactions where each transaction is verified by an extensive, decentralized network of computers.

On August 2008, bitcoin.org was registered and 2 months later October 2008, Bitcoin framework paper was published.

The paper was published by Satoshi Nakamoto. Satoshi is the founder and brainchild of Bitcoin birth. Although up to this date, no one knows the person's true identity although there are much speculations in the online community and the dark web arena. As far as we know, Satoshi is a brilliant and reclusive mathematician and was well versed in cryptography subject. Satoshi then made a final programming contribution in middle 2010 and then passed the reins to Gavin Anderssen which is Bitcoin's current lead developer.

Beta mining (2009 to 2011)

On January 2009, the bitcoin network comes into existence with the release of the first open source Bitcoin client and issuance of the first bitcoins.

Satoshi mined the first block of bitcoins ever, which had a reward of 50 bitcoins. This is famously known as the Genesis block.

Chapter 1: What is Bitcoin?

Following from October 2009, the first exchange rate was published at a rate of $1 to 1390.03 bitcoins and for the first time, bitcoins trade publicly. At that time, 1000 bitcoins were trading at $0.003.

True to its belief that Bitcoin existed, a Florida programmer by the name of Laszlo Hanycez made the world's first real Bitcoin transactions by spending 10,000 bitcoins to get two pizza delivered. This was made possible by enrobing his friend in England who then authorized his credit card order through the bank.

The world went abuzz on Bitcoin before it crashed (2011)

On June 2011, Bitcoin reaches its next breakthrough. The market peaks at the capitalization of $206 Million USD. However good things did not last. Mt. Gox which is the largest Bitcoin exchange in June 2011 which handled 90% of transactions traffic had their user information stolen from a hacker. 60,000 user details were leaked and of which, 600 had their Bitcoin balance stolen.

Promising future ahead (2011 to Present)

After the crash of 2011 by Mt.Gox, Bitcoin subject spent almost a year to regain the trust of its buyers. As it gains traction, more merchants accepted Bitcoin and trading started to pick up its tempo.

During April 2013, Cyprus government declare a bank holiday and decide to confiscate money from bank depositors and Bitcoin surge and double its value from USD $100 within 9 days and was trading at USD $200.

In November 2013, Bitcoin surges to over $1,000 per bitcoin. One bitcoin is now worth more than 300,000X as much as they did in the first public Bitcoin trade in 2010.

Over the last few six years, the currency has gone from being a mere experiment to a market capitalization of billions of dollars with 16 million market cap of Bitcoin now and a trading price USD$4500 per Bitcoin (August 2017)

While the future is not known, what is certain is that Bitcoin will continue to challenge the way in which people and governments think of money and how they define this new type of currency.

1.5 Bitcoin recognized as a currency

Besides Bitcoin trading had regarded Bitcoin as a commodity, Bitcoin also serves as an alternative

Chapter 1: What is Bitcoin?

payment method that can be used online or even offline. Bitcoin had been considered as a digital currency. By being in a decentralized payment method which denies any government, bank or any institution entity to control it. Bitcoin allows anyone in the world to accept this digital currency across any orders regardless what's the native currency the Bitcoin user is located. Besides, bitcoin can be transacted on mobile platform hence it is an alternative payment method to allow the user to use at minimum transactions fees.

For a while now, our society has been evolving towards the cashless arena. More and more people are using their bank, prepaid cards, debit and credit cards to pay for goods and services both online and offline and Bitcoin had been made a convenient currency tool, it allows Bitcoin user now turn to familiar-looking plastic which could be their prepaid Bitcoin card or even Bitcoin debit cards. Such plastic card can have topped up with Bitcoin. One successful example is Bitpay https://bitpay.com/card which allow their user to spend such digital currency like regular credit card and yet, having a clear ledger on their wallet by accessing the information online.

Now Bitcoin had been firmly rooted in modern finance by implementing block chain technology and is poised as a leader and example model in the future of currency and alternative payment system and certainly when Bitcoin evolve itself to currency or money, we certainly have to give the government its cut.

United States of America (USA)

The USA hosts the largest number of cryptocurrency users as of today, it also implies large Bitcoin trading volumes in the world. Silicon Valley is home to numerous cryptocurrency and currently the highest amount of Bitcoin ATMs presently in the world, United States has been at the foreground of embracing the digital currency from the very beginning.

As a global monetary superpower, many states across the globe look to the US, meaning they set the pace for other countries of the world. The US is undoubtedly serving as a testing ground for crypto-regulation. However, the government has had to brush shoulders with Bitcoin due to the illegal drug cartels who take advantage of the untraceable nature of the transactions in the network and FBI confiscated some accounts during the 2013-2015 growth period.

Chapter 1: What is Bitcoin?

China

China is dominating the Bitcoin network is creating concern as the world's second largest economy. China can be seen as a huge impact on the prices of Bitcoin globally as there's minimum government regulation exertion.

It is unclear how much money had moved out of China through Bitcoin and based on experts reports, 30% at least of today world's Bitcoin mining operations are done within China as cheap electricity is providing Bitcoin miners in China to maximize profit yield in comparison with other countries. In China northwest, Bitcoin miners are given low-cost wind and solar-powered electricity to set up Bitcoin mine.

Japan

In Japan, Bitcoin has, at last, gained the recognition of a mainstream currency ahead of other fiat currencies. The privilege given to Bitcoin follows the recent implementation of a new law in Japan which recognizes Bitcoin as a legal payment option within the country. This law went into effect on April 1, 2017.

However new law means that Bitcoin exchanges will inevitably come under additional regulatory scrutiny. The admittance of cryptocurrency as a legal tender means that the applicability of regulations governing banks and financial institutions in Japan will apply to cryptocurrency exchange platforms. The exchange platforms will be required to adhere to strict anti-money laundering (AML) and Know Your Customer (KYC) requirements, along with several mandatory annual audits.

1.6 Cryptocurrency debunked

What is a cryptocurrency? Cryptocurrencies are digital currencies that are not introduced by any financial institution or issued by any governments. Cryptocurrency has no intrinsic value but they share similar characteristic issued by the government. While normal currency issued by the government is treated as a legal tender, digital currency is a medium of change using cryptography.

Put in another simpler way for an average joe to understand, cryptocurrency is electricity converted into lines of code rated in the complexity of the work by hashing in exchange for a monetary value or in the simplest form for all to understand, cryptocurrency equates as digital currency.

Chapter 1: What is Bitcoin?

1.7 Cryptocurrency hashing

Cryptocurrency mining power is rated respectively in a measurement unit of hashes per second. A mining rig of 1KH per second(1KH/s) is mining at a rate of 1000 hashes in a second while a 1MH per second mining hardware is mining at a rate of 1 million hashes per second. Currently, the rate of measurement is H/s, GH/s, MH/s & PH/s.

Hashing uses an algorithm to solve a chunk of large information which is known as solving Bitcoin blocks.

1.8 Bitcoin hashing

A hash algorithm takes data of any formattable size which comes in the form of alphabets, numbers and transform them into a fixed alpha-numeric string. The output size can vary from 64-bit, 128-bit or even 256-bit.

Bitcoin hashing can be treated as a fingerprint of the data processed through the hash function because within the same output data can only be generated the value of input data. Should in the event if a hacker deliberately forces to alter the input value, the hash output will be completely changed.

In this context, Bitcoin adapt this blockchain technology as a consensus mechanism to secure all its transaction data.

1.9 What is Bitcoin block?

Bitcoin block represents a series of information from the past to present. Each block contains a record or all recent transactions. In Bitcoin mining context, it also contains an answer to the difficult mathematics puzzle and each block is a unique individual. Every mathematics problem is linked to every block so Miners are required to process and record the transaction as part of the mining process. Bitcoin mining is all about completing the existing "Bitcoin block" marathon to earn the Bitcoin.

A typical scenario in a Bitcoin mining is every time a Bitcoin block is completed, it will have its transaction record down in the network while it will make way for the next Bitcoin into the blockchain network. Such information is permanent as they will store the transactions record and such continuous cycle will allow all transactions data to be stored permanently within the blockchain network.

The blockchain network is not like a line segment which contains the source(roots) to the

Chapter 1: What is Bitcoin?

latest records but instead, it expanded and branches out like a tree-like structure. In figure 1.9, it explains the sequencing of subsequent Bitcoin get generated

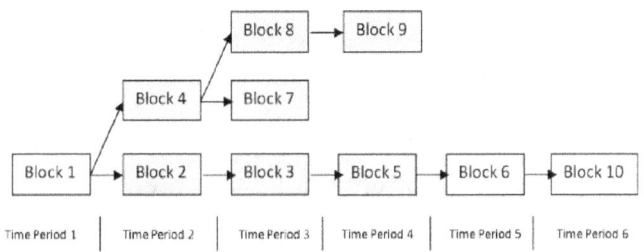

Figure 1.9

Once a miner solves this Bitcoin block, a new Bitcoin block of 12.5 bitcoin will be generated again. The total number of Bitcoin coin is capped at 21 million. In the starting phase of Bitcoin mining from the year 2008, per Bitcoin block contains 50 Bitcoin and was subsequently halved after every 210,000 blocks.

1.10 Blockchain explained

The blockchain is a term widely used to represent this new suite of technologies. Within a blockchain environment, all transactions are recorded chronigically which form an indestructible chain.

Mastering Bitcoin for Beginners

It is practically anonymous as all records or known as ledgers is distributed across many participants in the subscribed network so it doesn't exist in a singular place. There are always multiple copies existing in the network as all participants or known as the node are simultaneous.

The technology beside incorporating blockchain onto Bitcoin, blockchain be adapted to many applications which require a record of transaction data. These application examples are property titles, intellectual property, currency, digital signatures or even current currency and such application had been widely adopted by financial institution

Chapter 2:

Should You Invest in Bitcoin?

Many peers, even family members or close friends around me had asked me, why should they invest in Bitcoin even they know nuts about Bitcoin?

I want to get something out of the way first. Bitcoin is not a commodity like a stock or an entity but it's a currency. Just like our currency is money and now I sincerely ask, who doesn't love money? So when you invest in Bitcoin or advocate its use, you're buying the currency and believe this currency will work in your daily life.

These 5 hypothetical scenarios on a broader scale and my own explanation I will be providing;

Reason 1

Myth: You believe the US government's massive dollar printing program is causing global inflation?

Explanation: Since 2009, the US government has added an unprecedented $5 trillion to the total money supply. On the other hand, other governments around the world also increase their own money supplies to hedge their exports competitively supply.

Reason 2

Myth: Another financial crisis ahead?

Explanation: The financial crisis of 2008 by Lehman brothers cause over-leveraging of financial giant (banks or financial institution). Only after deleveraging in 2009, the leveraging was down to a ratio of 10:1. Currently, it's back to 31:1 ratio.

Reason 3

Myth: Could government "bail out" banks?

Explanation: As shared earlier on the history of Cryptocurrency and birth of Bitcoin. Cyprus bank accounts holder were treated by the government and in some cases, 70% of their savings were taken.

Reason 4

Myth: Do you have the real banking privacy?

Explanation: Unless you're in the tax haven of Switzerland and can afford to park your cash and investment, there will be no certain privacy, period.

Reason 5

Myth: You believe in flexibility

Explanation: In this technology era, we no longer keep our possession records through physical ledger but instead everything can be uploaded online. Email and the internet have too changed the way operate our life. Cryptocurrencies will have the same disruptive impact on finance industry and if bank does not shift

2.1 Why invest in Bitcoin?

The simplified way an average joe can invest in Bitcoin is either buy some or join Bitcoin mining pool and harvest them. Buying Bitcoin today is simpler than before as many established Bitcoin exchanges all over globally by provides buying and selling of Bitcoin services using your credit card.

For instance, if you're staying in the United States, Coinbase http://coinbase.com allow you to fuss-free purchase Bitcoin at a markup rate of 1% over the current market price. As an additional bonus, if you're a United States citizen, Coinbase has an easy option link up your United States bank account to your Coinbase wallet. Besides making it easier for USA citizens, it also allows their user to purchase Bitcoin on a recurring basis.

Is investing in bitcoin a good idea now?

As of August 2017, Bitcoin price had jumped to 1400% this year to record high at a price above $4,700. It is also understandable from the Bitcoin miner community that it is more profitable to mine Bitcoin while on the other hand, economists are speculating about where it goes next? The possibility of breaking the next barrier of $5,000 is nearing and it could power price towards the $15,000 in the new term.

So, what really makes bitcoins valuable?

While you let your thought sink in, let's consider why bitcoins are valuable? We had explored the benefits of Bitcoin –decentralized distribution,

Chapter 2: Should You Invest in Bitcoin?

ease of convenience without involving a middleman, a global network, an immovable blockchain and this list can go on but these fine features but not the real drive for this value hike in Bitcoin value.

What really makes Bitcoin valuable are two properties which are authenticity and scarcity.

✓ Scarcity

Bitcoin has similar value the same reason gold has value. People want this but there isn't enough to go around for everyone. New gold can't merely be created because one must find a gold mine and expensive process of refining the gold. The reason gold has served so well as money throughout the history is the combination is because of its scarcity.

✓ Authenticity

Gold has been used in money and had been universally associated with wealth. As we embark into a digital age, hundreds of cryptocurrencies label themselves as digital currency, therefore, it causes a problem against the claim of authenticity.

As of currently, Bitcoin holds the highest market capitalization and Bitcoin the largest of the network effect, therefore, is the most widely recognized so its real authenticity.

2.2 What does it really mean to invest in Bitcoin?

The first thing that came into my mind is you need to know your want and your risk appetite. The first question you need to answer to yourself is what do you want to **invest** in Bitcoin? Do you want to buy the currency and hoping it could appreciate over time or simply you want to invest because you're being told that Bitcoin is emerging as the next thing for 2017 and 2018 and you should jump onto it?

While you let your thoughts sink in, let me explain what's Bitcoin investment.

The most common form of Bitcoin investing is buying the currencies or any commodities as the lowest price and selling it at the highest price for the maximum yield in relatively in a short interval. There's always a saying "buyer buy low, seller sell high." In all scenario, you need to decide for yourself if it's a good time to buy.

Chapter 2: Should You Invest in Bitcoin?

To better understand Bitcoin and its current or previous price, the best place to find out the latest price is Bitcoin exchange. Similarly, if you want to invest in stocks or Forex, you refer to their respective exchange to understand the trading price.

These are the list of Bitcoin exchange you can refer to;

1) Coindesk https://www.coindesk.com

2) GDAX https://www.gdax.com

3) CEX https://cex.io

4) Kraken https://www.kraken.com

5) Bitcoinaverage https://bitcoinaverage.com

Here's the way how a typical online Bitcoin exchange works

1. You create up a basic account by providing your typical personal information and banking information

2. You would be directed to your email to receive a separate email on how to activate your account

3. Once the account is activated, you need to complete a verifications procedure

Know-your-customer(KYC)

In order to properly use and transact within a Bitcoin exchange, there's a need for the user to complete a "Know-your-customer" verification procedure. Some common personal information related to you will be required, this information includes

- ✓ Your personal identification issued by your country or maybe a copy of your driving license

- ✓ Recent utility bills or other proof-of - address

- ✓ Your phone number

Once such information had been submitted, there's a waiting period which typically takes about few hours to a day or two. Whenever you submit any documents, be sure that all information is clear and legible as it would expedite the verifications process by your respective Bitcoin exchange.

All exchange has indicators how the current market is doing and for the case of a Bitcoin

Chapter 2: Should You Invest in Bitcoin?

exchange, these prices can fluctuate by quite a bit, especially of lately where prices fluctuate. As we know the world of economics, supply and demand are based on the market and Bitcoins exchange allow Bitcoin buyer and seller to connect.

Most of the bitcoin exchange uses a software based trading engine which matches buying and selling orders on the two side and trading will take place once the user confirms the price. In recent years, the trading quantum and volume of Bitcoin has increased exponentially with most trading taking place in United states and China. There are two types of bitcoins exchanges in practice today. They are **PTP** and **Regular**.

- ❖ **PTP (Peer to Peer) exchanges**: A familiar acronym used in today. Some common applications are torrent applications which allow one relationship between the senders and receivers. Peer to peer exchange allows participants of the market to trade directly with each other without any third party to process the trades. All trades are operated and maintained exclusively by software.

- ❖ **Regular exchanges**: They are a medium between the buyers and sellers. The user can set or limit their orders to buy or sell bitcoins at a certain price they're comfortable with. The exchange will just find the best matching order once user accepts them

2.3 How Bitcoins exchange operates

Just like physical currency exchanges, you're essentially buying one currency with another. For instance, you can buy Thai Baht(THB) using the US dollar(USD), or you could be buying British pound using Japanese Yen(JPY). The same principle works for Bitcoin except the value come what traders perceive the value and the complexity of math equation required to mine Bitcoin. In other words, Bitcoin exchanges are a commodity trading platform.

That said, Coinbase.com or other typical exchange actually act as intermediaries for currency transactions which actually convert Bitcoin to your currency or vice versa by changing your dollars to Bitcoin. By exploiting the constantly shifting value of the various currencies, investors like you or me can make a tidy sum of profit by moving money around these markets all in the process known as arbitrage

Chapter 2: Should You Invest in Bitcoin?

The common payment methods accepted and used by most Bitcoin exchange are;

- ✓ Bitcoin transfers
- ✓ Bank wires
- ✓ Credit cards
- ✓ PayPal
- ✓ Liberty reserve
- ✓ International wires
- ✓ Money gram
- ✓ Western Union remittance services

2.4 How does a regular Bitcoin exchange really works?

On a regular transaction, people looking to sell bitcoins will specify the amount and price they would to sell them at. All such request known as orders are placed into a common ledger which calls the order book.

When a Bitcoin buyer logs in the similar platform, they will look into the order book to look for a satisfactory offer and if none can be found, the buyer can create a buy order specifying the terms they will like to have. Whenever possible, the Bitcoin exchange will try to match the buy and sell offers offered by a different party and process the trades once both users accept the prescribed terms. Once the buyer and seller agree to transact, the trade is completed.

Buying Bitcoin with real money

Here's a few warning I ought to remind you before you buy bitcoins physically with real money inside a Bitcoin exchange;

1. **Access your risk appetite:** never invest more than any amount you're not willing to lose

2. **Lock up your wallet**: once you have your own personal Bitcoin wallet to store your bitcoins, make sure you don't lose it. The safest way is to buy a hardware wallet to store your bitcoins physically. <u>More information on the type of wallet will be provided later.</u>

3. **Diversify it**: Don't put all your Bitcoin onto the same wallet. The high valued wallet is always the target for hackers. You

Chapter 2: Should You Invest in Bitcoin?

should have an online and offline wallet always.

4. **Watch the price**: Bitcoin is notoriously volatile that is the value can climb up or drop significantly over short time frames. Bitcoin buyer should keep an eye on the price charts and make a timely purchase when the price is right.

5. **Look out for the fees**: different bitcoins exchange has a different fee structure to suit various user patterns. Fees are typically a percentage of transaction amount

6. **Security**: When trusting a Bitcoin exchange with your money, ensure that their security measures are top of the line. Some common exchange price use two-factor authentications to safeguard their clients

An important point of Bitcoin exchanges is the fact that certain platforms allow you to exchange Bitcoin to your respective local currency. For instance, if you live in the states, you will want to get your hands into US dollars(USD), similarly, if you're staying in the European Union, you will want to trade with euros(EUR). A full list of website classifiable based on your location where you can buy bitcoins physically with real money, credit card, PayPal and bank transfer;

International

Bitsquare	https://bisq.io
Bitstamp	https://www.bitstamp.net
Bitwage	https://bitwage.com
Coinbase	https://www.coinbase.com
Kraken	https://www.kraken.com
Local Bitcoins	https://localbitcoins.com
Xapo	https://xapo.com

Europe(EU)

Anycoin Direct	https://anycoindirect.eu
Bitcoin.de	https://www.bitcoin.de
Rock trading	https://therocktrading.com
Paymium	https://www.paymium.com

Chapter 2: Should You Invest in Bitcoin?

BL3P	https://bl3p.eu
Bitpanda	https://www.bitpanda.com

Japan

Coincheck	https://coincheck.com
BTCBox	https://www.btcbox.co.jp
Bitflyer	https://bitflyer.jp

Australia

Bitcoin Australia	https://bitcoin.com.au
CoinJar	https://www.coinjar.com
Cointree	https://www.cointree.com.au
Hardblock	https://www.hardblock.net
Coinloft	https://www.coinloft.com.au

United

Kingdom

BittyLicious	https://bittylicious.com
Coincorner	https://www.coincorner.com
CoinFloor	https://www.coinfloor.co.uk

China

BTCC	https://www.btcchina.com
Huobi	https://www.huobi.com
OKCoin	https://www.okcoin.cn

2.5 How Bitcoin exchange works

Besides regular exchange, How does a P2P Bitcoin exchange works then?

Peer to peer exchange allows participants of the market to trade directly with each other without any third party to process the trades. The P2P Bitcoin software is capable to match traders without the need of any human intervention which edge as a decentralized trading platform

Chapter 2: Should You Invest in Bitcoin?

on cryptocurrency without having a single company in charge of things.

Benefits of P2P Bitcoin exchange

Additional benefits include full anonymity since such trading platform don't require a singular point of authority while on the other hand, it provides total anonymity since they don't have to go through any central point for transactions or authority which could be coerced by hackers or government. Besides the anonymity, P2P Bitcoin exchange offers cheaper operations as it again does not require a company to operate but the exchange of information is between people to people thus it lower down any transactions fee.

Most importantly, the P2P exchange does not work like regular exchange which provide escrows services and instead, the P2P exchange does not hold any bitcoin for their respective user but instead they connect traders together allowing them to trade directly.

As peer to peer exchange have a bigger role to play ahead of the years due to its vast advantage over conventional Bitcoin exchange, we shall take a look into the top 4 peer to peer exchange that is currently in the market

1. **Local bitcoins** https://localbitcoins.com/

   The go-to platform for peer-to-peer Bitcoin trading with its decentralized support. Besides having a substantial user base, it offers a standard fee of 1% whenever you place an advertisement to sell. There is a reputation based system inbuilt within the website which allows traders to gauge the other party reliability.

2. **Bit square** https://bitsquare.io

   Bitsquare offers an open source desktop type application available in Windows and Linux. Bitsquare allows trade without centralized control thus prevent any privacy issue or allow any central authority like banks, governments or other institution to access their user information. The trading fee is based on trade amount and distance to the market price.

3. **Bisq** https://bisq.io

   Bisq is a desktop based application that boosts they allow their user to start trading within 10 minutes. The application can be downloaded on the website and there's no Know-your-customer requirement which explains the benefit of instantly accessibility benefits

4. **Coinffeine** http://www.coinffeine.com

Coinffeine is hosted by different decentralized nodes meaning it is impossible to be shut down or censored. The founder of coinffeine touted his creation as BitTorrent of Bitcoin. Similarly, in all P2P Bitcoin exchange, trades are executed directly without any intermediary. It charges a 0.5% from the trade amount

2.6 Buying Bitcoin from ATM

Besides buying Bitcoin from online which we've covered earlier, you can purchase Bitcoin offline which is through Bitcoin ATMs

Bitcoin ATMs are like your regular ATMs but instead of spitting our local currency like dollars or euro, Bitcoin ATMs deliver Bitcoin to your wallet upon the insertion of cash.

There is a different type of Bitcoins ATM made by different companies at different countries. In general, some require proof of identification while some don't require any upfront verifications.

For ATMs that require verifications, the user is required to scan their national identification which the ATM will validate before the user can then feed in cash and in exchange, the bitcoin will be transferred to the bearers Bitcoin wallet address. On the other hand, certain ATMs generate a paper wallet or known as an offline wallet which is the bearer instruments of that bitcoins which are generated in the form of QR code onto the printed paper.

Bitcoin ATMs generally sell bitcoins at a markup rate 5% to 8% above the Bitcoin value. This markup fee is due to the infrastructure cost and maintenance – example of building an actual ATM and the backend stage required to transfer the money and bitcoins

So a good advice to all my readers is before walking up to your nearest Bitcoin ATM, do check against the current exchange price of Bitcoin.

Chapter 2: Should You Invest in Bitcoin?

To find your nearest Bitcoin ATM, you may visit https://www.buybitcoinworldwide.com/bitcoin-atms

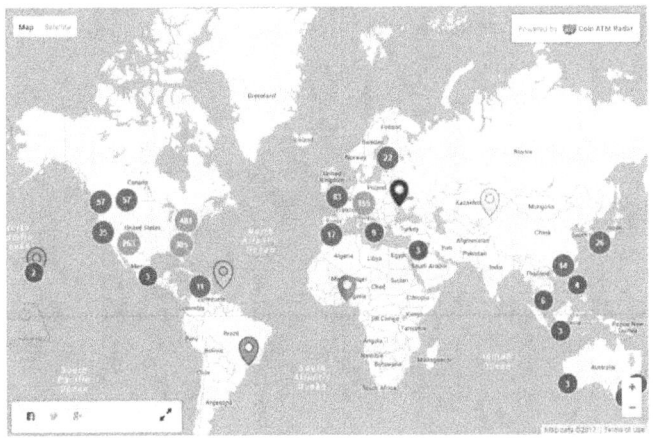

Source: buybitcoinworldwide.com

Chapter 3:

Bitcoin Mining

If you had not done your homework, this book is your go to the material as I will walk through with you that you do not really need to invest a real dollar in return for Bitcoin but instead you could mine Bitcoin from the next few following pages.

It's a simple 4-step approach which can be easily implemented within 1 week and you will be laughing yourself to the bank in the near future when Bitcoin price continues to appreciate over time.

3.1 Introducing Bitcoin Mining

New bitcoins are produced by a vast network of computers that whir away at cracking difficult math problems to validate other Bitcoin transactions. Bitcoin is known as a cryptocurrency because encryption techniques are used to create bitcoins and to exchange them and every exchange is embedded with a certain level of encryption. Every transaction is added to a public ledger called the blockchain. The process of running a program to solve these problems is called mining.

An algorithm that controls the complexity of the math problems to be solved caps the total number of bitcoins produced at 21 million. The closer the total bitcoins mined comes to 21 million, the more complex the math problems that are created and the more processing power computers need to solve them.

Today(August 2017), 16.5 bitcoins are in circulations that had been mined which are 78% of the total possible supply. Miners need customized rigs designed to do nothing but solve blocks of Bitcoin problems. Miners usually join forces with a pool of other miners. A reward of 25 bitcoins goes to the miner or mining pool that solves a block first, something that occurs roughly every 10 minutes.

Bitcoin mining in the early days

In the earliest days of Bitcoin, mining was done with CPUs from normal desktop

Chapter 3: Bitcoin Mining

computers. Graphics cards, or graphics processing units (GPUs), are more effective at mining than CPUs and as Bitcoin gained popularity, GPUs became dominant.

In fact, in the early days of Bitcoin mining, the miner will be rewarded with a total block of 50 bitcoins but as the mining pool continue to remain while more miners joined the fray, the block got splits between the miners. At the time of writing, the current Bitcoin block reward is 12.5 bitcoins which will be halved in a few years from now.

Many people were just running normal PCs during the early days or using old CPU with recent graphics cards, and they could earn a few Bitcoins every day.

Back in the day when I was using my CPU and GPU for bitcoin mining, I was mining 20 bitcoins every 3 days in 2012 and it was profitable if I had the foresight to keep the Bitcoin until now where each Bitcoin was translating up to $4,700 per bitcoin.

Eventually, hardware known as an ASIC, which stands for Application-Specific Integrated Circuit, was designed specifically for mining bitcoin. These microchips computers were created for one purpose which is to mine bitcoins.

The first ones were released in 2013. These devices became economically futile and were designed to run just for application on cryptographic calculation algorithm and the most powerful of them which is SC Mini rig have the efficiency of 1,500 Gh/s. with the increase of Bitcoin efficiency mining power, Bitcoin miners shifted from being a hobby and fun side project to considering serious commercial scale with a monetary benefit on returns.

3.2 Understanding how Bitcoin mining works

Bitcoin mining is not just about generating additional bitcoins. Mining also adds records to the public ledger which is part of cryptocurrency blockchain because in every blockchain application, all transactions need to be recorded in that block of data and that block of data has to be done by Bitcoin miners.

Bitcoin mining had become an intensive resource and tedious process over the last few years as more people is competing to mine the Bitcoin block which thus raises the mathematical equations. By increasing the Bitcoin

Chapter 3: Bitcoin Mining

mathematical equation then the flow of new bitcoins can remain at a steady growth at every ten minutes' interval which explains why it is possible to calculate the last year when the last block of bitcoin could be mined because Bitcoin is supply capped at 21 million coins.

Lastly, you have to understand that without Bitcoin miners existence, no bitcoins could be bought into the market for use or circulation but what stops most is the electric charges and investments cost to set up a proper mining operation.

3.3 The 22% balance mining

Now you may ask me, what's left of the pie is only the 22% of bitcoin pool readily available for mining and is it worth mining? My answer would be it depends on how much you're willing to spend and how much you're able to hold the bitcoin while waiting for Bitcoin to appreciate over time.

Each person you ask may provide you different opinion depending on their own factors (capital cost, operating cost, electricity rate, etc.). Again this is to each own's risk appetite and their perception of Bitcoin in the future (i.e.:

possibility of Bitcoin price inflation from current price of $4,700 to $5,000 or even $10,000)

For a more realistic approach to find out if mining is profitable with your current factors, you can refer to Bitcoin mining profitability calculators which were invented.

These mining calculators take into several variables such as

- ✓ Cost of your hardware
- ✓ Electricity cost
- ✓ Hash rate of your hardware
- ✓ Power consumption
- ✓ Current USD to Bitcoin exchange rate

3.4 Calculating mining profit

To calculate all these parameters, we will take a simple mining calculators from 99bitcoins.com

Chapter 3: Bitcoin Mining

Difficulty factor	923233068449	
Hash rate	Hash rate	TH/s
BTC/Block reward	12.5	
USD/BTC exchange rate	4752.9350	
Pool Fees %	Leave blank if not sure	
Power (Watts)	Leave blank if not sure	
Power Cost (USD/kWh)	Leave blank if not sure	
Hardware Costs (USD)	Leave blank if not sure	
	Calculate mining profit	

Figure 3.4: Bitcoin calculators' engine from 99bitcoins.com

To explain on the Bitcoin mining terms, you should get to know

❖ Difficulty factor

Earning is based on the current difficulty to mine bitcoins. As this is an exponential growth, Bitcoin difficulty factor will usually increase as times goes by

If you're unsure what's the value of difficulty factor, do leave it as what it is.

❖ Hash Rate

The Hash Rate is the rate at which these problems are being solved. The more miners that join the Bitcoin network, the higher the network Hash Rate is.

The Hash Rate can also refer to your miner's performance. A higher hash rate is better when mining as it increases your opportunity of finding the next block and receiving the reward.

Several measurements to measure the hash rate and they are;

1. H/s (hash per second)
2. MH/s (Mega hash per second)
3. GH/s (Giga hash per second)
4. TH/s (Terra hash per second)
5. PH/s (Peta hash per second)

❖ Hardware cost

Just like any business, there's always an upfront cost or hardware cost that is required. Good miner hardware is expensive.

Chapter 3: Bitcoin Mining

ASIC miner which stands for ***Application-Specific Integrated circuit*** is designed specifically for mining bitcoin. ASIC miner beta version was released in 2013 and had been improved over time.

The ANTminer S9 is currently the most efficient miner and cost USD $2000 and you can mine approximately 0.4 bitcoins per month which translate up to USD $1880 worth of bitcoins per month. To put it simply, it will take approximately 2.5 months to break even.

During purchasing of any hardware, you will want to consider the entire efficiency metrics which is measured from H/s to PH/s. A higher hash rate means more powerful miner.

Always remember that buying a Bitcoin miner that has low watt to hash rate is the key for any profitable mining operations.

❖ **Energy cost(USD/kWh)**

Electricity cost can make or break any mining operations. Below is the average residential rates by US states in 2016.

Always remember to factor in the energy cost as it will make or break your mining operations

Mastering Bitcoin for Beginners

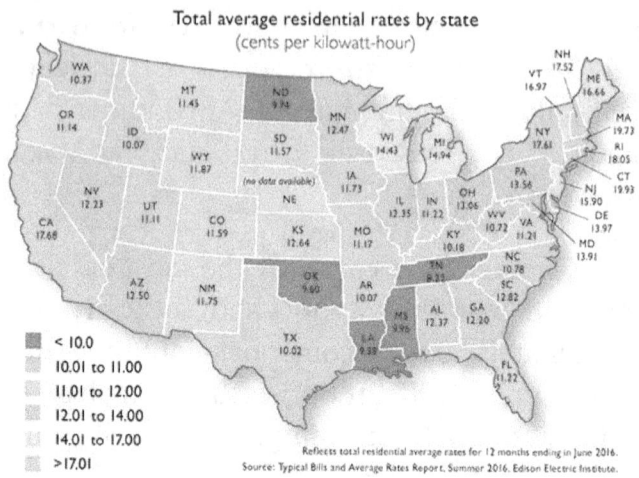

Figure 3.3.3 Rates by state
Source: https://www.rockymountainpower.net

❖ Power consumption – Watts

Each miner consumes a different amount of energy. Be sure to find the exact power consumption of the miner before even calculating your mining profitability. This information is usually supplied at point of purchase.

3.5 ASIC mining hardware comparison

Below are the stats on Bitcoin mining performance using ASIC hardware. They are sorted based on the product name, the Advertised Hash rate per second, the Hash to

Chapter 3: Bitcoin Mining

Joule, their power watts and the current price, its current market availability and what type of communications port.

* CPU and GPU are not included in the below table as product performance may vary from vendor and model variance.

Appendix table 1

Product	Advertised Mhash/s	Mhash/J	Watts	Price (USD)	Currently shipping	Comm ports
AntMiner S1	180,000	500	360	299	Discontinued	Ethernet
AntMiner S2	1,000,000	900	1100	2259	Discontinued	Ethernet
AntMiner S3	441,000	1300	340	382	Discontinued	Ethernet
AntMiner S4	2,000,000	1429	1400	1400	Discontinued	Ethernet
AntMiner S5	1,155,000	1957	590	370	Discontinued	Ethernet
AntMiner S5+	7,722,000	2247	3,436	2,307	No	Ethernet
AntMiner S7	4,860,000	4000	1,210	1,823	No	Ethernet
AntMiner S9	14,000,000	10182	1,375	2,400	Yes	Ethernet
AntMiner U1	1,600	800	2	29	Discontinued	USB
AntMiner U2+	2,000	1,000	2	17	Discontinued	USB
AntMiner U3	63,000	1,000	63	38	Yes	USB
ASICMiner BE Blade	10,752	129	83	350	Discontinued	Ethernet
ASICMiner BE Cube	30,000	150	200	550	Discontinued	Ethernet
ASICMiner BE Sapphire	336	130	2.55	20	Discontinued	USB
ASICMiner BE Tube	800,000	888	900	320	Discontinued	Proprietary
ASICMiner BE Prisma	1,400,000	1333	1100	600	Discontinued	Proprietary
Avalon Batch 1	66,300	107	620	1299	Discontinued	Ethernet, Wifi
Avalon Batch 2	82,000	117	700	1499	Discontinued	Ethernet, Wifi
Avalon Batch 3	82,000	117	700	1499	Discontinued	Ethernet, Wifi
Avalon2	300,000			3075	Discontinued	USB or Ethernet
Avalon3	800,000				Discontinued	USB or Ethernet
bi*fury	5,000	1,176	4.25	209	Discontinued	USB
BFL SC 5Gh/s	5,000	166	30	274	Discontinued	USB
BFL SC 10 Gh/s	10,000			50	Yes	USB
BFL SC 25 Gh/s	25,000	166	150	1249	Discontinued	USB
BFL Little Single	30,000			649	Discontinued	USB
BFL SC 50 Gh/s	50,000	166	300	984	Discontinued	USB
BFL Single 'SC'	60,000	250	240	1299	Discontinued	USB
BFL 230 GH/s Rack Mount[18]	230,000			399 (used)	Discontinued	USB
BFL 500 GH/s Mini Rig SC	500,000	185	2700	22484	Discontinued	Wifi
BFL Monarch 700GH/s[19]	700,000	1428	490	1379	Yes	PCIe, USB
BitFury S.B.					Discontinued	RPi GPIO

Mastering Bitcoin for Beginners

Appendix table 1 Cont

Model					Status	Interface
Bitmine.ch Avalon Clone 85GH	85,000		650	6489	Discontinued	Ethernet, Wifi, USB
Black Arrow Prospero X-1	100,000	1000	100	370	Discontinued	Ethernet
Black Arrow Prospero X-3	2,000,000	1000	2000	6000	Discontinued	Ethernet
Blue Fury	2,500	1000	2.5	140	Discontinued	USB
BTC Garden AM-V1 310 GH/s[21]	310,000	954	324	309	Discontinued	RPi GPIO
BTC Garden AM-V1 616 GH/s[21]	616,000	951	648	350	Discontinued	RPi GPIO
CoinTerra TerraMiner IV	1,600,000		2100	1500	Discontinued	Ethernet
Drillbit					Discontinued	USB
HashBuster Micro	20,000	869	23	688	Discontinued	USB
HashBuster Nano					Discontinued	USB
HashCoins Apollo v3	1,100,000		1000	599	Discontinued	USB
HashCoins Zeus v3	4,500,000		3000	2299	Discontinued	USB
HashFast Baby Jet	400,000	909	440	5600	Discontinued	Ethernet, USB
HashFast Sierra	1,200,000	909	1320	7080	Discontinued	USB
HashFast Sierra Evo 3	2,000,000	909	2200	6800	Discontinued	USB
Klondike	5,200	160	32	20	Discontinued	USB
KnCMiner Mercury	100,000		250	1995	Discontinued	Ethernet
KnC Saturn	250,000	400	300	2995	Discontinued	Ethernet
KnC Jupiter	500,000	400	600	4995	Discontinued	Ethernet
KnC Neptune	3,000,000	1429	2100	12995	Discontinued	Ethernet
LittleFury					Discontinued	USB
Metabank	120,000	705	170	2160	No	
NanoFury / IceFury	2,000	800	2.5		Discontinued	USB
NanoFury NF2	3,700	740	5	50	Discontinued	USB
Red/BlueFury	2,600	1040	2.5	640	Discontinued	USB
ROCKMINER R3-BOX	450,000	1000	450	200	Discontinued	USB
ROCKMINER R4-BOX	470,000	1000	470	210	Discontinued	USB
ROCKMINER Rocket BOX	450,000	937	480	599	Discontinued	RPi GPIO
ROCKMINER R-BOx	32,000	711	45	65	Discontinued	USB
ROCKMINER R-BOX 110G	110,000	917	120	88	Discontinued	USB
ROCKMINER T1 800G	800,000	800	1000	325	Discontinued	USB
Spondooliestech SP10 Dawson	1,400,000	1120	1250	2845	Discontinued	Ethernet
Spondooliestech SP20 Jackson	1,700,000	1545	1100	1309	Discontinued	Ethernet
Spondooliestech SP30 Yukon	4,500,000	1500	3000	4121	Discontinued	Ethernet
Spondooliestech SP31 Yukon	4,900,000	1633	3000	2075	Discontinued	Ethernet
Spondooliestech SP35 Yukon	5,500,000	1506	3650	2235	Discontinued	Ethernet
TerraHash Klondike 16	4,500	140	32	250	No	USB
TerraHash Klondike 64	18,000	140	127	900	No	USB
TerraHash DX Mini	90,000	140	640	6000	No	USB
TerraHash DX Large	180,000	140	1,280	10500	No	USB
Twinfury	4,500	1174	3.83	216	Discontinued	USB

Source: https://en.bitcoin.it/wiki/Mining_hardware_comparison

3.6 Calculating non-specialized hardware for Bitcoin mining

Do you know besides the given specifications of ASIC mining hardware, you can also find

Chapter 3: Bitcoin Mining

specifically your non-specialized hardware CPU or GPU performance?

A simple resource tool I always refer to will be at

- https://www.nicehash.com/?p=calc
- https://en.bitcoin.it/wiki/Non-specialized_hardware_comparison

Bitcoin mining in desktop based hardware

Why is Bitcoin mining no longer practical using non-specialized hardware?

CPU's and GPU's are horribly inefficient compared to ASIC's. considering any GPU's in 2014 or before, they cannot out perform any ASIC given the current Bitcoin difficulty rate.

There are generally two GPU manufacturers that provide the chips for all today graphics card which is NVIDIA GeForce or ATI Radeon and it turns out that Radeon card is much efficient mining hardware than NVIDIA cards. It is believed the difference in the card's architecture that makes ATI a better successor in Bitcoin mining.

Some GPUs have a higher hash rate than others, while some guzzle up more electricity. In the old days before 2015, Bitcoin miners always had difficulty in finding a balance between power and the electricity but given the significant improvement of ASIC mining hardware over time, it is inevitable that to mine Bitcoin in the most efficient way today is to invest in ASIC hardware only.

However, for my readers who still believe that mining with non-specialized hardware could be their starting point given the assumption they have such hardware in their home PC, they may like to explore the following graphic card options.

Radeon R9 295x2

The Radeon R9 have a hash rate of 46MH/s and will cost you $449 on Amazon

Radeon Rx 480

The Radeon Rx 480 has a hash rate of 25MH/s and will cost you $119 on Amazon

Chapter 3: Bitcoin Mining

3.7 Choosing Bitcoin ASIC Bitcoin miner hardware commonly used

Application-specific integrated circuit chips (ASICs) are Bitcoin mining hardware created solely to solve Bitcoin blocks. They have just negligible pre requisites for other typical PC.

As Bitcoin mining increments in notoriety and the Bitcoin value rises so does the estimation of ASIC Bitcoin mining equipment. As more Bitcoin mining equipment is conveyed to secure the Bitcoin arrange the Bitcoin trouble rises. This makes it difficult to contend without a Bitcoin ASIC framework beneficially. Moreover, Bitcoin ASIC innovation continues getting quicker, more effective and more profitable so it continues pushing the cutoff points of what makes the best Bitcoin mining equipment.

For a quick snap on the best, ASIC Bitcoin hardware options are(not in efficiency or economic order), refer to figure 3.7

Mastering Bitcoin for Beginners

AntMiner S7	AntMiner S9	Avalon6
Advertised Capacity: 4.73 Th/s	**Advertised Capacity:** 13.5 Th/s	**Advertised Capacity:** 3.5 Th/s
Power Efficiency: 0.25 W/Gh	**Power Efficiency:** 0.098 W/Gh	**Power Efficiency:** 0.29 W/Gh
Weight: 8.8 pounds	**Weight:** 8.1 pounds	**Weight:** 9.5 pounds
Guide: Yes	**Guide:** Yes	**Guide:** No
Price: $479.95	**Price:** $1,987.95	**Price:** $499.95

Figure 3.7 – top 3 ASIC based hardware

Chapter 4:

Bitcoin Wallet

What is Bitcoin wallet?

If you had read the earlier chapters, you'll notice there's plenty of mention about Bitcoin wallet. So you could be asking yourself, "what is a bitcoin wallet? "in this chapter, we'll reveal all!

As the name suggests, a bitcoin wallet is a wallet that you can store all your bitcoins. Besides the primary role that serves as a tool to store your bitcoins, it also serves as a platform for you to send and receive funds – similar to a bank account.

There's no exaggeration that a bitcoin wallet is the most important thing to safe keep our Bitcoin and digital currency.

Mastering Bitcoin for Beginners

Beyond the functional role of storing, sending and receiving bitcoins, every Bitcoin wallet will come with a unique set of bitcoin address which is a private key.

4.1 What is the private key?

The private key on your Bitcoin wallet is the most important piece of information. They are a set of the 256-bit key in hexadecimal which ranges from 0 to 9 or A to F and 64 characters long.

A typical sample bitcoin private key

E8873D79C6D87DC0FB6D5778633389F445321 3303DA61F20BD67FC233AB83262

Without knowing the corresponding private key, funds that are stored in a Bitcoin wallet cannot be spent. Even with reverse engineering onto the wallet is total impossible thus this makes Bitcoin one of the toughest encryption built to date and it's totally impossible to crack.

Should one day your encryption for Bitcoin private key be compromised, it will be advisable to send it to a different wallet that seems more secure. Fundamentally the concept of bitcoin is it can only be spent once and cannot be reversed

Chapter 4: Bitcoin Wallet

thus once the amount is spent, the private key that becomes useless.

4.2 Different type of Bitcoin wallet

Now as we understand what's the functional role of Bitcoin wallet and how secure your Bitcoin could be, we'll explore the different variety of Bitcoin wallet that is available. In summary, there are several options you can store your Bitcoin. Variety of example choices is also provided in their respective category.

Desktop wallets: A software Bitcoin wallet is a software based Bitcoin application that stores its data onto the specified computer hard disk. When any software based wallet is installed onto the computer, it would create a log file(wallet.dat) which will hold the data of your Bitcoin wallet.

		Windows	Mac OS	Linux
Bitcoin Core	https://bitcoin.org/en/download	Yes	Yes	Yes
Bitcoin KNOX	https://bitcoinknots.org/	Yes	Yes	Yes
Electrum	https://electrum.org/	Yes	Yes	Yes
Green Address	https://bitcoin.org/en/	Yes	Yes	Yes
circuit	https://arcbit.io/	Yes	Yes	Yes

BitGo	https://www.bitgo.com/	Yes	Yes	Yes
Msigna	https://www.bitcoin.com/choose-your-wallet/msigna	Yes	Yes	Yes
Armory	https://www.bitcoinarmory.com/	Yes	Yes	Yes
Bither	https://bither.net/	Yes	Yes	Yes

Table 4.2.1 -Table of available desktop wallet

Mobile wallets: An app based wallet that can function on your mobile phone. Besides it's most convenient in today mobility world, it can be functioned on Apple iOS and Android, it can be used on Blackberry platform too. Besides its handy features functioning on a mobile phone, it can be applied on instant payments via QR code

	is	Android	**Blackberry**
Bither	Yes	Yes	-
Breadwallet	Yes	Yes	-
GreenAddress	Yes	Yes	-
Airbitz Bitcoin wallet	Yes	Yes	-
BTC.com	Yes	Yes	-
Coinbase	Yes	Yes	-
Bitcoin wallet	-	Yes	Yes

Table 4.2.2 – Table of Mobile wallet for Bitcoin in different mobile OS

Chapter 4: Bitcoin Wallet

Online Web wallets: Cloud based services provided by third party companies. All transaction requires internet connections

Coinspace	https://coin.space
GreenAddress	https://greenaddress.it
BitGO	https://www.bitgo.com
BTC.com	https://wallet.btc.com
Xapo	https://xapo.com
Coinbase	https://www.coinbase.com

Table 4.2.3 – Table of Online web wallets that are powered by cloud based

Paper wallets: Alternatively, also known as cold wallets. Offline wallets that are not connected to the live blockchain so it's not "active" Refer to chapter 4.6 "fun exercise to create a new Bitcoin paper wallet"

Hardware wallets: A hardware based Bitcoin wallet which is stored onto a physical, portable device. This is also another form of cold wallet. To use any Bitcoin store in this hardware, the user needs to connect it to the internet. You may like to note that the prices quoted as per table exclude any shipping charge.

Coinspace	https://coin.space
GreenAddress	https://greenaddress.it
BitGO	https://www.bitgo.com
BTC.com	https://wallet.btc.com
Xapo	https://xapo.com
Coinbase	https://www.coinbase.com

Table 4.2.5 – Table of available hardware wallets for Bitcoin

4.3 Cold Wallets and its advantage

Paper wallets or dubbed as offline wallets or cold wallets is the most secure method of holding your bitcoins. As when a Bitcoin is transferred from an address, they are stored in the blockchain but to be able to spend them, the

Chapter 4: Bitcoin Wallet

private key is required. Thus, a paper wallet is the most secure way of holding your Bitcoin.

A good tip during creating a paper wallet is to make sure you're not connected to the internet. As we know if you're connected to the internet, there's a chance malware could copy your record, record your private key and access them onto your Bitcoin address at a later date.

4.4 Explaining Bitcoin address

A Bitcoin address is an identification which contains 26 to 35 alphanumeric and beginning with 1 or 3. It is a Bitcoin designation for any Bitcoin payment. Any creation of Bitcoin address can be generated at absolutely no cost.

There are currently two address formats in circulation now, P2PKH and P2SH

- ✓ Pay-to-Pub-key-hash(**P2PKH**): Common P2PKH will have number beginning with 1

    - ➢ 1CvBMSDYstQetqTFn5Au5m4GFg9xJaNVN3

- ✓ Pay-to-Script-hash(**P2SH**): Newer P2SH type will have number starting with number 3

➢ 3GCHMvV3i2k3G15jZtkRxWWCjq ZQeW6HC1

A Bitcoin address is a single use token just like one-time pin however they are a different concept. All Bitcoin user has a different address which is accompanied with their private key. Most Bitcoin company offering Bitcoin services will have such free services to generate a new address whenever a new payment request is required.

4.5 Bitcoin address balance

If you're unsure whether your Bitcoins address had received any funds or did your transaction to transfer funds had been successful or query how many Bitcoin you have in your bitcoin address, you can query this against the blockchain network by simply going to https://blockchain.info

Summary		Transactions	
Address	1N:Nja1bUmhSoTXcvzBRBEtN8LeF9T	No. Transactions	436
Hash 160	ae2dd6a6b295ace7f4f90e958fe5dcffdf73b505	Total Received	36.21864609 BTC
Tools	Related Tags - Unspent Outputs	Final Balance	36.21864609 BTC

Figure 4.5.1 A typical Bitcoin address balance and the total number of transactions taken place

Chapter 4: Bitcoin Wallet

Besides querying your current Bitcoin balance, you can also query against the type of transactions which is similar to your internet banking where you can query against your last transactions.

Every bitcoins transaction will come with a transactions ID number you can refer to. The transfer's details which include amount sent, sender and receiver Bitcoin address as well date of transfer can be found in the block chain. Such information is publicly available since this is how Bitcoin blockchain framework works.

Typically, the recipient will ask the sender to provide their Bitcoin address and transactions ID to verify against their record so each party at both ends could confirm on their Bitcoin transactions.

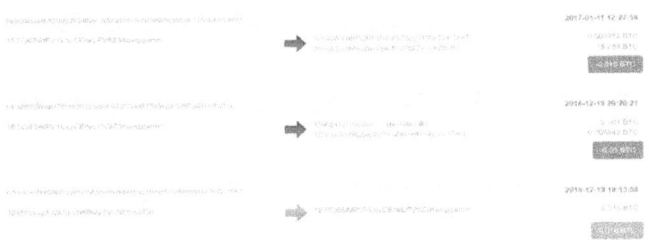

Figure 4.5.2 Bitcoin transaction reference

Mastering Bitcoin for Beginners

4.6 Fun exercise to create a new Bitcoin paper wallet

Skip all the boring stuff and do something fun now, shall we? Let us generate some instant bitcoin address by typing in random text and moving your mouse pointer onto your computer screen. Here is the step-by-step guide to setting one up.

> **Step 1**: Visit http://bitaddress.org

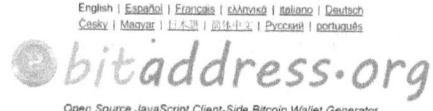

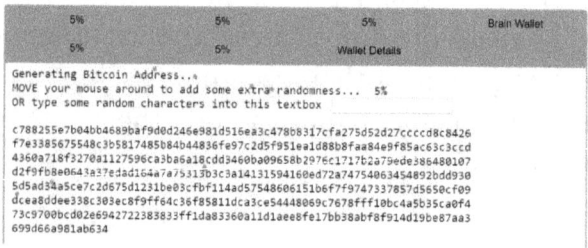

> **Step 2**: The above figure should be like what you see on your screen now. Enter some random text in the text box move around your mouse cursor within the screen. You should notice the progress bar is increasing

Chapter 4: Bitcoin Wallet

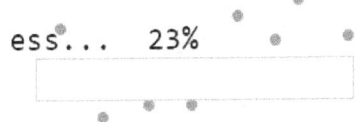

ess... 23%

- ➤ **Step 3**: wait for the progression of Bitcoin wallet to complete, you should be assigned to the Bitcoin Wallet and Private key with QR code

- ➤ **Step 4**: Besides generating a single Bitcoin Wallet in https://bitaddress.org, you can also create Paper Wallet, Bulk Wallet, Brain Wallet, Vanity Wallet and Split wallet

!!!! Additional note you must always remember !!!

- ✓ Should you wish to print the QR code out, please ensure it's being safely kept in a zip lock bag to guard against any wear and tear or water damage.

- ✓ Separate your Bitcoin address and Private key altogether! *You don't keep your ATM*

Pin by printing it onto your ATM card, don't you?

- ✓ You're solely responsible for generating the Bitcoin address and the associated private key so make sure you're **only** one who can access to those details only

Before you sign up any Bitcoin wallet with any Bitcoin third party to make or receive payment, be sure to understand it is always your responsibility to adopt good practices to project your money which is like, in real life, your wallet should always be with you all time. Some good practice includes;

- ✓ Diversify your wallet by keeping them separately instead of lumping them into one wallet

- ✓ Back up your wallet

- ✓ Encrypt your online backups to guard against online malware or hacker

- ✓ Make regular backup on a regular basis to synchronize latest balance and transactions

Chapter 5:

Bitcoin Mining Pool

What is Bitcoin Mining pool?

Pooled mining is a mining approach where numerous producing user adds to the era of a piece and afterward split the reward agreeing the contributed handling power. Pooled mining viable decreases the granularity of the square era compensate, spreading it out more easily after some time.

With a mining pool, many individuals add to solving a bitcoin block, and the reward is then distributed among them as indicated by their mining pool. Thusly, rather than sitting tight for a considerable length of time to create 12.5 Bitcoin in a block, a shared mine worker may get a small amount of a Bitcoin.

Today we will show you a few parts of pool mining with the expectation that they will enable you to pick a mining pool that best fits your necessities.

You can look at the mining pool reference in https://www.cryptocompare.com/mining/#/pools. Make sure to read the reviews and to check their features carefully. You will also find a list of servers by location and coin in the pool description.

5.1 Choosing a Mining Pool

There is a wide range of mining pools accessible. Which one you pick relies upon an assortment of variables. Would it be a good idea for you to join the biggest pool conceivable, to augment your possibility of a reward? It doesn't work that way. On the off chance that you join a huge pool, your likelihood of effectively mining a piece as a major aspect of the pool increments, yet the span of the pool implies that your payout will be lower. Everyday payouts will be more unsurprising.

On the other hand, if you are a piece of a little piece in the pool, at that point you will effectively mine blocks lesser. When you do, however, your reward will be higher. Thus, you may go at some point without acquiring anything, and after that get a vast reward. Over time it will all standardize.

Chapter 5: Bitcoin Mining Pool

Mining Pool Options

- **Single vs multi-coin pools:** Some cryptocurrency pools focus on one virtual currency, like Bitcoin. Mining different coins in view of which one they believe are most beneficial at the time. They utilize different components to choose this, including the hash rate of the pool at the time, and the rate of trade between various coins.

- **Local vs cloud mining:** Some mining pools combine cloud-based mining with pooled activity. This means that you don't have to buy mining equipment at all but can simply pay for an online mining contract that is automatically woven into the pool. This minimizes your capital outlay but means that you must pay for your mining capability from your pool profits.

- **Payout options:** Pools pay out in various ways. Some pay participants immediately based on every 'share' that they successfully submit. A share is a valid piece of the mathematical puzzle that has been solved. That puts more risk on the operator of the mining pool, because shares may be earned even if the whole puzzle is not solved. The operator may end up paying out rewards for shares, even if they don't earn a reward from the blockchain. Over time there are many different payment systems that had been developed. Most Bitcoin mining vendors use the proportional or Pay per last N share(**PPNS**) but there are still several payment methods.

5.2 Type of mining pool payout

The pool pays as many shares as it can every time a block is found, prioritizing recent shares. Since the probability of finding a block is always the same

> ### ➤ **DGM (Double Geometric Method)**

A Geometric reward type that enables to operator to absorb some of the variance risks.

> ### ➤ **POT (Pay on target)**

Pays out accordingly based on the difficulty of work returned to the pool by a miner, rather than the difficulty of work done by the pool itself.

Chapter 5: Bitcoin Mining Pool

> **SCORE (Score based system)**

A proportional reward weighed by miner time submitted and rewarded with a proportional reward

> **PPLNS (Pay per last N share)**

Mirror of proportional payout, however, the operator will be eligible for a proportional payout if they get disconnected if it's no fault of their own

> **Proportional**

A reward is distributed among all miners proportionally based on the amount of bitcoins shares being found

5.3 Slushpool mining

Getting started with Bitcoin pooling using SLUSH POOL

In this part, you will learn how to start bitcoin pooling using SLUSH POOL(https://slushpool.com)

Slush pool is the first publicly available mining pool which was announced in 2010 under the registered name as Bitcoin pooled mining server.

Mastering Bitcoin for Beginners

Slushpool beside allowing the user to mine bitcoin, it also allows the miner to mine Zcash(ZEC). It has a well-arranged dashboard and a customizable payout point and has coin bonus with accurate and fair hashing weighting.

In Slushpool, Bitcoin can be mined for a 2% transaction fee while ZEC mining is tentatively free. The minimum pool payout for Bitcoin is 0.001 Bitcoin

Before you start, you'll need

- ✓ ASIC miner hardware
- ✓ Mining software
- ✓ Bitcoin wallet & address
- ✓ Email address

> **Step 1**

Sign up a new account on slush pool, wait for a confirmation email

> **Step 2**

Download **CGminer** (http://ck.kolivas.org/apps/cgminer) or **BFGminer**(https://bfgminer.com) software from the respective website

Chapter 5: Bitcoin Mining Pool

> **Step 3**

Unzip using WinRAR to open the archive and unpack it onto your hard drive

> **Step 4**

Configure your device

Your miner must be pointed to one of the stratum servers below and user credentials for your account have to be specified.

For your login details, you require your user ID and miner name in the format of "**userID.workerName**" so for example my userID is abc123 and my miner name is John789, the userID I will need to create will be "**abc123.John789**"

For slush pool server's location, there are 4 services location currently so select based on your geographical location

Servers Location	Address to be entered
USA, east coast	**stratum+tcp://us-east.stratum.slushpool.com:3333**
Europe	**stratum+tcp://eu.stratum.slushpool.com:3333**
China, mainland	**stratum+tcp://cn.stratum.slushpool.com:3333**
China, mainland	**stratum+tcp://cn.stratum.slushpool.com:443**
Asia-Pacific/Singapore	**stratum+tcp://sg.stratum.slushpool.com:3333**

➢ **Step 5**

On the very same setup page, Set your wallet address. This address is a unique identifier given to you when you setup a bitcoin wallet.

➢ **Step 6**

Chapter 5: Bitcoin Mining Pool

Once you have filled everything in, click start mining button. You can refresh slush's pool homepage and you will see your earnings.

5.4 Antpool mining

Getting started with Antpool, an alternative Bitcoin mining pool

Based in China and operated by Bitmaintech which is a soft company of Bitmain which also create Bitmain Antminer ASIC series. Bitmaintech is one of the respected Bitcoin mining manufacturers. Antpool is a Chinese Bitcoin mining pool and has a substantial Bitcoin mining network. It was created in March 2014 and have attracted more than 30% of bitcoin miner into their network.

Antpool had already established itself as one of the main players within the Bitcoin mining arena because they make it easy for everyone to get on board by finding their mining block at their own choice. Besides offering its miner a mining pool using Pay-per-last-N-shares(PPLNS) with a 2.5% fees, a Miner can opt for solo mine using your mining hardware with a 1.0% fees.

Mastering Bitcoin for Beginners

Besides supporting Bitcoin mining, Antpool offer supports of Ethereum and litecoin using stratum protocol.

Before you start, you'll need

- ✓ ASIC miner hardware
- ✓ Mining software
- ✓ Bitcoin wallet & address
- ✓ Email address

> **Step 1**

Sign up a new account on Antpool at https://www.antpool.com/home.htm, wait for a confirmation email

> **Step 2**

Download **CGminer** (http://ck.kolivas.org/apps/cgminer) or **BFGminer**(https://bfgminer.com) software from the respective website

> **Step 3**

Unzip using WinRAR to open the archive and unpack it onto your hard drive

Chapter 5: Bitcoin Mining Pool

➢ Step 4

Configure your device

Your miner must be pointed to one of the stratum servers below and user credentials for your account have to be specified.

For your login details, you require your user ID and miner name in the format of "Sub-account.WorkerID" so, for example, my sub-account is xzy123 and my work ID is pipe345, the ID I will need to create will be **"xzy123.pipe345"**

do note the sub-account and worker id must contain letters and numbers.

For slush pool server's location, there are automatically routed to their closest location which is currently located in the United States, Germany, Shenzhen, Beijing, Hong Kong and many more locations they got to offer. The stratum pool URL are stratum.antpool.com:3333, stratum.antpool.com:443, and stratum.antpool.com:25

Chapter 6:

Mining Hardware

Choosing your ASIC mining hardware

Application-specific integrated circuit chips (ASICs) are Bitcoin mining hardware created solely to solve Bitcoin blocks. They have just negligible pre requisites for other typical PC.

As Bitcoin mining increments in notoriety and the Bitcoin value rises so does the estimation of ASIC Bitcoin mining equipment. As more Bitcoin mining equipment is conveyed to secure the Bitcoin arrange the Bitcoin trouble rises. This makes it difficult to contend without a Bitcoin ASIC framework beneficially. Moreover, Bitcoin ASIC innovation continues getting quicker, more effective and more profitable so it continues pushing the cutoff points of what makes the best Bitcoin mining equipment.

Mastering Bitcoin for Beginners

Today, we're going to cover how to set up Antminer S9 as an example.

6.1 ANTminer S9

Bitcoin ASIC miner – Bitmain ANTminer S9

Overview

The Bitmain ANTminer S9 is composed of 189 ASIC chips across 3 mining boards, which are cooled by two loud powerful 120mm fans The total hash rate of the S9 is roughly 12 to 14 TH/s

The S9 is standalone mining hardware so it does not require an external controller however it does not come with a power supply.

In this part, we'll walk through with you how to easily set up your ANTminer S9

Chapter 6: Mining Hardware

Before we start, you'll need

- ✓ AntMiner S9 hardware
- ✓ 2 x 110v Power supply unit(PSU), rated at 1000W each or 1 x 220V Power Supply unit, rated at 1600W or above
- ✓ AngryIP software http://angryip.org
- ✓ Bitcoin Wallet & Address
- ✓ A Bitcoin mining pool account (refer to topic: **Getting started with Bitcoin pooling using SLUSH POOL)**
- ✓ Desktop or laptop
- ✓ LAN cable

Part 1: Connect your Power supply unit + LAN cable

> Step 1: Connect the power supply unit power cable connectors to each of the nine PCI-e connectors on the top of the AntminerS9 and ensure each hash board is powered by same Power supply unit(applicable for user using 2 x 110V PSU)

➢ Step 2: Connect power cable connectors to the Antminer S9 PCI-e connector on the controller

➢ Step 3: Connect your PSU to the wall outlet

Part 2: Setting up the Antminer S9

➢ Step 1: Connect Network Ethernet cable to the network port on Antminer S9, make sure your Antminer S9 is connected to the same network via router

➢ Step 2: Open AngryIP software to scan for your Antminer IP address

➢ Step 3: Open the Antminer IP address in your internet browser. The default userID and password is " root "

➢ Step 4: Go to the admin tab and change your userID and password if necessary

➢ Step 5: Go to the Miner Configurations tab, enter the stratum/IP address of your mining pool. This should have covered in the earlier guide for SLUSH POOL

➢ Step 6: Save the settings for your configuration. The set up will take a

Chapter 6: Mining Hardware

couple of minutes to connect to the mining pool

➢ Step 7: To check if the connection is live, go to the Status page to see the live status of your Antminer S9

Chapter 7:

Bitcoin Usage

Way(s) to use Bitcoin

As you had learned what is Bitcoin, how Bitcoin mining works so you should now know how to spend or use Bitcoins because bitcoins can be used in a different application in our life. As Bitcoin steam across the value, it's no doubt the popularity and acceptance driven by awareness of users and merchants.

To my very perspective and proved by statistic and results, the hottest investment in the world today is Bitcoin. The rush of Bitcoin has been very recent. With Bitcoin price trading at $4,700 per bitcoin now, the 2 pizza that was bought in 2010 with 10,000 bitcoins is now worth $47 million dollars now.

7.1 Your brick and mortar store

Bitcoin increase publicity of your local shop in multiple ways and therefore it helps to boost your sales, exposure through word of mouth within the Bitcoin communities.

No currency is required and most of the Bitcoin merchants do not charge any processing or handling fees.

To find your nearest Brick and mortar store within your communities, you can go to CoinMap https://coinmap.org

Bitcoin as an investment vehicle portfolio

As we know Bitcoin has its supply capped at 21 million coins which are expected to complete by 2140, there are ample opportunities to make a long term investment in Bitcoin.

IRS treats Bitcoin as property when they recently issue guidance stating that virtual currency as federal for federal tax purpose while in the Asia region, Japan accepted Bitcoin as a legal tender on April 2017

There is growing number of Americans who believe the growth and potential of Bitcoin thus putting their savings on Bitcoin as their

Chapter 7: Bitcoin Usage

retirement plan in hoping the value of bitcoins will appreciate and grow substantially over time.

The most important takeaway is investing in Bitcoin should be a part of a long-term plan and not treated as a short-term gain as Bitcoin is still in the early stage of development and require more education to drive awareness onto individual as an investment opportunity so to let the price of each bitcoin be appreciated.

Use bitcoin to further study

The University of Nicosia, a private school of Cyprus is the first university to accept bitcoin for their tuition fees.

Besides accepting this new cryptocurrency as a form of payment, this university is also proposing the world's first "Master of Science Degree in Digital currency". This move underscores that Bitcoin is driving into the mainstream of first cryptocurrency being accepted beyond small merchants.

7.2 Fly with Bitcoin

Besides buying your daily essentials from Bitcoin accepted merchants like food, clothes, electronics, event tickets, you can now also use Bitcoin to buy flight tickets using your Bitcoin

This website https://www.btctrip.com allow bitcoins owners to exchange their bitcoins in favor of the perfect vacations

As the website says motto says " flying with bitcoins " is the perfect way to describe how Bitcoin had evolved to a currency that can be accepted as a mode of payment onto the high-value item.

Vacation with Bitcoin

Now you've completed your flights shopping through BTCtrip, you can now possibly shop for your favorite lodging. Be it a penthouse in new York city or a villa stay in Bali because Expedia is accepting bitcoins.

Expedia https://www.expedia.com is one of the largest online travel agencies and since June 2014, holidaymakers have the options to make payment for their hotel using bitcoins.

Bitcoin payment is applicable to hotel booking as of now but there are plans for payments for your flights or even activities

Chapter 7: Bitcoin Usage

7.3 Gambling with Bitcoin

We caveat against this and do not suggest our reader using this approach, however, should our reader insist and wish to explore the options, you've been warned

The As different country may recognize gambling may or may not be legal so before you do anything first, check your local law and regulations first.

Assumedly if online gambling is legal where you are located, bitcoins can offer an alternative growth on your existing Bitcoin balance. Most gambling site using Bitcoin as payment does not require your personal details. Simply synchronize your Bitcoin wallet with them and you can start playing.

We know you're sensible and responsibly grown up but we would like to end off to remind you to gamble responsibly.

7.4 Bitcoin trading with rare metal

Besides being an investment instrument, Bitcoin can allow the user to purchase precious metals such as gold or silver.

There are various platforms to allow user trade against Bitcoin with these precious metals. There is some great success story we learned from the community while some simply don't meet the break-even point.

The top trading platform is Vaultoro which is primarily located in United kingdom and hedge against real 100% gold which is stored inside their professional vault. They provide statements each month to your own tracking and tax purposes. Should you wish to bail out from this investment portfolio, they offer to install settlement back to Bitcoins.

You can visit Vaultoro
at https://www.vaultoro.com or alternatively, you can refer to other merchants like Uphold at https://uphold.com or BitGold
at https://bitgold.com

7.5 Trading Bitcoins for shopping gift card

There are several sites which offer you to trade in your bitcoins in exchange for a gift card which you can further spend on Websites like Amazon, eBay, Macy, Nike, Sephora, Target and other internationally recognized merchants.

Chapter 7: Bitcoin Usage

In exchange of your bitcoins for the gift card, you can do your shopping using them as such merchants does not accept Bitcoin payments directly at time of writing. Besides redeeming for your own use, you can also gift such gift cards to your loved one during the festive season.

To shop with gyft at https://gyft.com, it's only 3 steps away to pay with Bitcoin!

Step 1: Choose your desired gift card you wish to purchase.

Step 2: Select Bitcoin as your preferred payment.

Step 3: Send payment through your Bitcoin wallet during check out.

7.6 Converting your Bitcoin to cash through Bitcoin ATM

According to Bitcoin ATM charts provided, there are about 45% of installed Bitcoin ATM facility actually support sell operations. To find your nearest Bitcoin ATM, you can go to https://coinatmradar.com/.

There are currently 1525 Bitcoin ATM across the globe spread across 58 countries so it should be convenient for Bitcoin owner to exchange their bitcoin for cash even when they are vacationing.

In general, there are several stages that all user need to follow.

- ➢ Stage 1: Verifying stage where the user is required to identify themselves with national identification.

- ➢ Stage 2: Once the verifying is done, you can now send the bitcoins to the specific ATM's Bitcoin address or some may provide QR code for the easier application.

- ➢ Stage 3: Depending on the ATM operation setting, you may withdraw cash immediately or may take up to 24 hours and thereafter, they will be notified through SMS and re-invited back to the same ATM to withdraw the cash.

7.7 Shopping Bitcoins' Search engine

Finding the best product and website that accept Bitcoin can be a challenge, isn't it? Afraid not, Spendabit https://spendabit.co allow you to browse through a catalog of 3 million item that you can purchase with your Bitcoin.

Chapter 7: Bitcoin Usage

The search engine crawls through multiple e-commerce platforms or merchants so they will address to most of your shopping needs.

Spend a bit platform not only allows you to browse through items easily but you can sort according to pricing factor, merchants and even by region. Price will be appeared in USD and further converted to bitcoins once you enter into the respective merchants check out page.

Crowdfunding with Bitcoin

Crowdfunding has gained popularity over the years and StartCOIN https://startjoin.com have taken the advantage by allowing start up and capitalist communities to fund on concepts, ideas, and projects.

StartCOIN is a reward based coin which rewards their user for pledging, sharing and holding StartCOIN. The more you share and support in StartCOIN, the more StartCOIN you will receive.

7.8 Donating your Bitcoin for charitable cause

Feeling generous or Thanksgiving near the corner? Besides receiving a gift, should you also consider gifting to the less privileged ones or gifting for the organization for fighting a better humanity or improving poverty communities?

For charity purpose to help within the non-profit United states communities or even sub-Saharan Africa communities who suffer from lack of access to clean water, you can visit https://bitcoinforcharity.com

Alternatively, you can donate your Bitcoin to organizations for Arts, Entertainment, NGOs or even net-politics. For the full list of organizations that accept bitcoins for donations, please visit https://en.bitcoin.it/wiki/Donation-accepting_organizations_and_projects

The above example is not exhaustive as there are more companies will be making the switch to Bitcoin payment. Most big businesses had already taken Bitcoin and integrated Bitcoin in their payment process and payment processors like bitpay or coinbase.

Small businesses are not excluded as well because much local brick and mortar store are making the switch. While greater usage on Bitcoin remains to be explored, there are often more unexpected benefits for merchants who had embraced them. In the next chapter, we'll explore what's the key takeaway and benefits for merchants who switch to such Bitcoin payment processor.

7.8 How to be a Bitcoin merchant

Bitcoin could be the cure to the problem of global currency where ledger is centralized and some cashless payment type transactions fee is being borne by payee or payer.

An estimated of 200,000 business today globally already accept Bitcoin today. These forward-thinking merchants of all business size and variety of trades are accepting Bitcoin payment trends. Besides the benefit as an alternative payment trend, it also helps business owners to cut cost on card fees while their customer enjoys a variety of benefits as well.

If you sell things in a brick and mortar store, your customers can pay using hardware terminals, touch screen apps or simply scanning your store QR code in their app digital wallet. QR codes are the biggest help in real world bitcoin transfer between consumer to consumer, business to business or customer to business or vice-versa.

For online Bitcoin payment, accepting Bitcoin is not much of a challenge in today as third party support company like Bitpay https://bitpay.com enable Bitcoin payment in your e-commerce website and receive a settlement for Bitcoin payments directly to your bank account.

By subscribing to Bitpay payment processor services, it brings Bitcoin payee and payer closer while bridging any complexity for Bitcoin merchants to cash out in their respective bank when customer make payment in bitcoins.

Benefits of accepting bitcoin for your business

There are many reasons that small business or e-commerce site should be accepting bitcoins as payment. Read on below for the few reasons you should.

1. The integration is simple, quick and lost cost. Sometimes certain Bitcoin merchants even offer no cost fee for business merchant start up

2. Your customer does not need to bring cash or do you need to bring the cash into the bank because bitcoins are directly paid into your digital wallet

Chapter 7: Bitcoin Usage

3. The payment between your customer and your digital wallet is instant and there is no-charge back

4. As a payee, you incur no charges while your customer only pay a small transaction fee which usually amounts up to USD0.01

5. You keep more of your money because credit cards take up to 3% of processing fees on every transaction

6. Your customer will be assured their personal information or credit card information which usually is required to process the payment will not be stolen as Bitcoin payment is anonymously

For a starter, we'll recommend BitPAY https://bitpay.com as your supporting company on Bitcoin transactions because BitPay allows you to accept payment in Bitcoin and receive fund directly to your designated bank account. Currently, they are partnered with 33 countries and offer up to 150 different currencies and provide your global clients a selection of up to 40 languages

Besides its banking convenience in online presence to transform your Bitcoin from your digital wallet and into cash in your favorite bank, offline Bitcoin merchants can simply accept a payment but enter an amount and your customer will just scan the QR code that the BitPay app generates.

Before we forget, if you accept Bitcoin as a payment method, it's a good idea to publicize it. Letting the crowd, they can spend their Bitcoin will help you drive your business sales and bring the bitcoins rolling in.

Put a Bitcoin Logo on your website or your shop front

Download the images "Bitcoin accepted here "and resize it if necessary. Besides putting this Bitcoin logo on your website, you can print it onto window decals and put it your shop front to alert cryptocurrency user that Bitcoins are welcome as a mode of payment.

Bring awareness through online presence

"Free advertising, why not?" This is the common quote I get from a business owner who just plunges into the Bitcoin payment bandwagon.

Advertising is a great way to promote their website or business and get some traffic and to add in the idea that it's a free advertising, it's an

Chapter 7: Bitcoin Usage

advantage for Bitcoin merchants while on the other hand, Bitcoin user will know which merchants honor their bitcoins.

Below are the few places you could practically place your business listing as a business accepting Bitcoin.

- ✓ Coinmap.org
- ✓ Spendbitcoins.com
- ✓ Yelp
- ✓ Bitcoin subreddit
- ✓ Create a website

Chapter 8:

Bitcoin Sutra

Technology has really shifted the way how to do just everything in our lives which means the way we consume data and information. Researching or finding more information on Bitcoin and other digital currency is evolving could be daunting as information is widely available however there are quite a few resources are at your disposal all of which are expected to bring you updated information on the bitcoin and its ecosystem.

These websites will provide information on Bitcoin pricing, trading patterns, current market capitalization and other variety of subjects.

1. Bitcoin.org

https://bitcoin.org

Mastering Bitcoin for Beginners

The mother of Bitcoin community or the home page of Bitcoin. This website resource provides short demonstration video to guide novice user and walk through in brief over Bitcoin subject. This portal is a great way to educate Bitcoin starters without overwhelming them.

2. Bitcoin Wiki

https://en.wikipedia.org/wiki/Bitcoin

A Wikipedia section dedicated for Bitcoin subject because it offers facts with an independent source of Bitcoin information. It offers its own explanation on Bitcoin technicality and breaks down them in finer details.

3. Coindesk

https://www.coindesk.com

Coindesk is one of the top few resources you can turn to for up-to-date news and information on digital currencies and blockchain technology.

Besides news and information, you can find Bitcoin price in their Bitcoin pricing index which is a measurement of Bitcoin performance. Information can be referenced to the early stage of Bitcoin from 2010 to present. Besides the line chart, you can refer to, you also have the option to view it in open-high-low-close(OHLC) chart or usually known as candle stick graph which is a professional tool as it serves illustration on Bitcoin movement in the price of a financial instrument over time.

4. Multiple News sites

Keep yourself updated on any news is the correct practice you should adapt to if you wish to invest in Bitcoin. There is specifically news site that is dedicated to this subject of Bitcoin, cryptocurrency, and blockchain.

You can visit all them here

- ✓ https://www.coindesk.com
- ✓ https://cointelegraph.com
- ✓ https://coinjournal.net
- ✓ https://news.bitcoin.com
- ✓ https://www.cryptocoinsnews.com

Do note the list is not exhaustive but serve my reader as a reference guide only.

5. Bitcoin forum

https://bitcointalk.org

Mastering Bitcoin for Beginners

One of the popular places for bitcoins beginner, enthusiast, expert, miner, programmer, trader or the even general public. Besides forum user communicating English for the main section, there are sub forums in other langue like French, Dutch, Russian, Italian, Turkish or even Chinese.

If you wish to participate in the forum, all you need is to register an account on the forum. Topic covered within the forum could entail trading Bitcoin to off topic like asking the user what their biggest fear is. So be sure you're into the sections of the forum when asking your question.

At the time of writing, there are 1.08 million forum users with a daily registration of 400 new users per day and average post of 7500 per day.

6. **Mainstream media coverage**

When it comes to mainstream media coverage on Bitcoins, it usually portrays that Bitcoin is not a good investment tool and encourage people not to invest in Bitcoin in fear that it is a balloon and may burst anytime but given the recent tremendous rise in Bitcoin price, it is no doubt mainstream media is driving a different direction altogether.

Chapter 8: Bitcoin Sutra

Besides as a Bitcoin enthusiast, it's more heartening to see more coverage on this topic as it creates more awareness across the globe. More and more people are already aware of Bitcoin and mainstream have to continue to keep up this momentum of such topic coverage if they want to remain relevant

7. YouTube or any interactive media

Over the years, more informational videos had been created by Bitcoin enthusiast due to this disruptive virtual currency which created a lot of media sensation and speculations. Such enthusiast main purpose is to drive awareness on Bitcoin because if more people believe in cryptocurrency, the value of bitcoin will continue to grow. Besides, it allows the viewer to understand how Bitcoin works visually(less the boring words) and how bitcoin can and will, one day, change the world.

Chapter 9:

Conclusion

Final words from the author

No one knows for sure whether Bitcoin could become the mainstream currency or will its popularity decline.

At the initial stage of Bitcoin during its evolution phase, it was initially perceived that cryptocurrency was a tool of crime, used within vice activities while it met onto several bumps by mismanagement of Bitcoin exchanges and wallet services but all these were mooted to early adopters that understand the vast implications.

As the market capacity for cryptocurrencies grows so will their stability. Once that happens, bitcoin will have the potential to be more stable than any currencies. Historically, the currency had been extremely volatile but given its recent boom, it will definitely hit beyond $10,000 or maybe $500,000 by 2030, who knows? So nabbing a fractions of the Bitcoin definitely look more enticing.

I see the next 5 to 10 years' future of Bitcoin as a series of reaction just like a line of dominoes where many of the next steps are dependable by the previous titles. So for now, try as much as possible to involve yourself with Bitcoin. Be it reading this book, reading mainstream media, participating in Bitcoin forum, or whatever activities that involve bitcoins because Bitcoin is a guaranteed growing currency.

Remember that Bitcoin worth is not the same as when it hits the market in 2008 and we know it won't be the same in 5 years or 10 years to come so let's be part of this cryptocurrency evolution journey in the next 5 years' time!

Now if you think you enjoyed this book and learn something new or interesting, please feel free to drop an honest review within the sales channel that you've purchased this book from. Alternatively, you may spread this wealth of information to your loved ones at the next meet up or through Social Media.

I wish you well and successful in your Bitcoin journey in 2017 and beyond!

www.ingramcontent.com/pod-product-compliance
Lightning Source LLC
Chambersburg PA
CBHW050109230526
45470CB00004B/1751